NIGHT CRIES

THE WESLEYAN POETRY PROGRAM: VOLUME 80

"Sawest thou ever thy friend asleep? Wert thou not dismayed by thy friend looking so? O my friend, man is something that hath to be surpassed."

— NIETZSCHE

MICHAEL BENEDIKT

NIGHT CRIES

WESLEYAN UNIVERSITY PRESS

MIDDLETOWN, CONNECTICUT

The author thanks the Creative Artists Public Service Program of New
York State for grant support during the writing of this book.

Acknowledgement is gratefully made to the following periodicals, in the pages of
which some of the prose poems in this book were first published: *Ambit, The
American Poetry Review, Arion's Dolphin, Black Warrior Review, Dada-Surreal-
ism, The Falcon, Fiction, Fiction International, Field, The Ohio Review, The Paris
Review, Partisan Review, Tri-Quarterly, and Unmuzzled OX.*

Library of Congress Cataloging in Publication Data

Benedikt, Michael.
Night cries.

(The Wesleyan poetry program: v. 80)
I. Title.
PS3552.E54A17 1976   811'.5'4   75–32526
ISBN 0–8195–2080–2
ISBN 0–8195–1080–7 pbk.

Manufactured in the United States of America
First edition

CONTENTS

5

I. The Night Cries

Night Cries

It's a cry in the night. Is it an animal being whipped, or two lovers mutually reaching their peak? In any case, it's a cry all right, but whether of pleasure or pain, so far it's been impossible to tell or say.

The Sarcophagus of the Esophagus

You always thought it was such a fertile place for expression of the human spirit. Great ideas and all, all taking root there —that kind of thing. But suddenly all you could hear were voices calling out, "Mama, Mama, take care of me"; or, in some cases, "Papa, Papa!" And, since there was seldom any satisfactory reply to this request, the human voice became bitter. Disappointment grew shrill as Hope. Everybody began to walk around making speeches about deprivation, trying to outshout his or her neighbor. People began to shout out things like "The world owes me a living!", even while calculating on possible burial benefits. Now it is only considered healthy if each person cries a lifetime before he dies. So if I meet you sometime, don't start out by speaking to me in poetic tones about the richness of words anymore, speak to me first about the sarcophagus of the esophagus.

The Death of the Human Particle

I was just sitting here at my desk quietly reading and, I thought, minding my own business, when I came upon an article containing the information that the cells in my body are dying by the millions every few minutes — 3,128,422 every minute was the exact figure. Also, the piece said that even should we just ever so slightly touch something, the poor things become bruised by the billions. Of course, it also explained, the body keeps replacing the extinguished cells, or otherwise each individual, such as the reader, would instantly begin to dwindle away and disappear. That was certainly a comforting thought, I thought but still, it was somewhat disconcerting to learn that even when I wave hello to my loved one as she approaches, by inviting her to wave back, I cause her to kill a million of her particles by accelerating the pressures of the air; should I greet her with a big kiss and a hug, I murder an entire generation; and should it fall out that we fuck, we practically commit utter cellular genocide. What kind of humanists are we anyway, we human beings whose existence produces only tragedy with even the most sympathetic of our gestures? And what kind of moralists are we, too? How can we go on after finding out a thing like this about ourselves, except by telling ourselves that we needn't worry; that since the body contains an infinite number of individuals, this decreases the importance of each one: or worse, perhaps we will justify our future slaughter by saying that it doesn't matter in the least how many cells we kill, since in a healthy person each dead individual cell is instantly replaced, and therefore no individual cell has any importance whatsoever. No, no, every man of true feeling knows that human life is an absolute; every man of true feeling knows also that whenever a single cell dies, it is appropriate that mankind cries; that to be decent the mourning ought to be general and universal, and the funeral home be crowded to capacity; that the line of honorary pallbearers should stretch as far as the furthermost horizon, while entire peoples get drunk at the wake; and as if by some earnest song or poem on one of the many serious subjects relating to the welfare of all mankind, the whole world be deeply touched.

Explanation of the Dark

Blackest night: A pack of animals is coming down the street, hair by hair! Where are they going to? You'll never know until you feel the fuzz brush up against your throat you'll find out from fangs; damp paws, dear child, will elucidate you

Cirrhosis of the Liver
for Dr. Martin Bax

Only a mother should be asked to suffer what he did to his liver; nonetheless, he worried so much about it that before long it took on the character of a daughter; in his imagination it was dressed up in a little wig, and the scars all became smiles in the morning when she gurgled so sweetly in his early embrace, and his emotions of affection flowed like pure, untroubled running water. How well he remembered its childhood, its growing years which went by so swiftly — almost too swiftly, he wistfully thought — full, incredibly rich years in any case. How much time they spent together, how very close they were! There were of course other beneficial friendships in her early youth, however; her close connection with her next-door-neighbor, Little Miss Kidney; not to mention her sympathetic responses, which caused all the neighbors pleasure, to a certain vagrant and mysterious creature who used to drift around the neighborhood, and who some said would have died without her solicitations: her first and favorite pet, "Pituitary." How they used to love to run along together through the forests of flesh, along with another forest creature, that veritable domesticated beaver, the ever-active Pancreas, with whom she would continuously go swimming. . . . And then, in the midst of all these thoughts, a fact was thrown up to him by fate; surely there would come a time when one day she would slip into her grown-up clothing, a sheath of peek-a-boo net design; and some day soon after, he reflected, full of bitterness, she would meet a promising young man of medical bent, a date would be set up between them, and she would be taken out. . . .

A Gift

It's a specially designed pistol for committing suicide, with a muzzle at one end and on the other a bottle-opener, in case you should decide to drink yourself to death.

Mother's Ingrown Toenail Phobia

Let me warn you: Most traditional mothers warn you against smoking, drinking, masturbating, and bad companions, in roughly that order; but some, like mine, warn you against ingrown toenails. After years of warning my brother and myself against their evils, advising us to cut our toenails regularly, and telling us that she "prayed to God we would never get them," it seemed only logical one Sunday when we actually caught her on her knees in front of the portrait of the Virgin Mary in the bathroom, beside the nail scissors, actually praying that we would never get them. Soon she took the next logical step: she threw away her little silver cross and began to wear a tiny nail-clipper on the gold chain around her neck. But did we ever follow her suggestions? And were they effective? All I can say is that after a while we all began to cut our nails regularly, twice a day; that I arrived here in my study to write this after hours of stumbling in the direction of my desk, stomping along on the stubbles of my footstumps; and that I'm writing this on a typewriter using my knuckles as fingertips.

The Criminal Animal

Human mothers are right to take such exceptional care of
their babies: after all, even from birth, there is no animal
which is quite like Man even as a child, Man differs from
the babies of other species. Yes, I know what everybody with
an I. Q. of over 43 during some period or another of unjust
war is thinking: that Man is quite a unique animal because
he is the only one to make war on his own kind, the swine.
But, believe me, my children, he is unique even earlier, and
for other reasons, otherwise he might never have survived to
become the only creature to make war on his own kind.
Unique first of all is the voice he uses to summon attention,
or invoke aid. Consider: whereas one laughs for joy at the
mew of a very young kitten, the peeping of chickadees, or
the squawking of the monkey—not to mention the mum-
bling of the baby elephant, the snort of the childish alligator,
or the harmonious warblings of the little whale or wren—the
human baby gives off the most extraordinarily earsplitting
shrieks and cries. Extraordinary by comparison, certainly;
because whereas the cry of other babies provokes mirth or
amusement, think back for a moment: Whenever a human
baby begins to cry, in some public place, at a meeting, or in a
moviehouse or at a football game, aren't the reactions to that
particular cry those of nearly universal annoyance, anger,
disgust, and even hatred? This is only to say that unlike the
cry of other babies, who attract attention by generating sym-
pathy, the human baby, up to a relatively late age, attracts
attention because human beings want desperately and in-
stantly to quiet his outcry. Thus we can see that the mature
human being is not only a murderer, as you say, but that
baby is a born blackmailer; and that from the perspective of
all the other creatures in the ecology, even the most un-
spoiled human cry must seem sinister. Although sentimen-

talized in a billion bad songs and/or poems, you can't fool the composers of nursery rhymes, which experts have shown are full of nothing but violence, murder, mischief and crime! That baby's playroom should be decorated with decals of baby lambs, bears, porcupines, giraffes or other creatures from the peaceable kingdom of the animals is as unjust as it is outrageous not to mention inaccurate! Like Lady Macbeth crying to hide her crimes, we protest too much with such insistence on our innocence, with our vision of children as cherubs! If only as a corrective, what we should really begin to picture on the walls of baby's playroom are pictures of Adam and Eve tearing their hair out as they exit from Paradise; Lucifer falling out of the sky and roasting his balls in hell ideally, Junior should be called Hitler.

The Statue of Fabric

What if the whole earth were actually only one enormous shoe, and the purpose of our feet were merely to enable men to walk around a bit on it, so as to explore its tremendous leather deserts? What if our pants were watching us, so that in order to assert our modesty we needed to undress? In that case, socks would be holes we would have to watch out not to fall in, the belt a pit, and the tophat a tunnel; and the well-known military servicecap an inverted trench into which we leap and crouch whenever we want to go out for a stroll, and in which, ostrich-like, we hope to hide our heads from horror. Oh, look, over there in the corner of this picture, hundreds of outright victims of clothing are being carried off in their heavy overcoats, kicking and screaming; only everybody imagines that overcoats actually offer protection, and blames it on the wind. How strange that buttoning up their fancy body-line-design shirts, men should feel as though their fat were under perfect control, and that they are therefore better equipped to pursue their independent destinies, when actually even the finest and most carefully pressed cloth is only a landing-stage, and a preparation for old age to first set foot on the body, where it will arrive like a sinister smuggler carrying its heavy cargo, our initial wrinkle. Believe it or not, I've known even confirmed nudists who were deluded, who dreamt of a bow-tie that would snap directly onto the throat, when what the wise sunbather really ought to realize is that even here it is a question of clothing that clutches as it clings, a question of a throat that will find itself snapping onto a bow-tie, and that nobody can ever be vigilant enough. For everywhere we can see that it is the day which dresses us and not the reverse, we awake every morning to carry this unstable statue of ourselves on the way to work, this Statue of Fabric into which we happen to fit; when we awake every morning it is already secretly dreaming of the day when it will topple over and crush all the dead life out.

Food for Sight
or, The Beginnings of Bacchanalia

We believe in preparing our food attractively, so attractively that sometimes it seems a shame that, to get the usual benefit from it, we actually have to consume it. And even have to grind it down again, so it becomes invisible! Before dining now, our preparations are so complicated, it's as if we believed the eye were some kind of secret stomach, or as if intestines had vision. When we're even a little hungry, it's as if that meant our digestive juices were giving a wink in the direction of our liver. And it's as if the anal canal were nothing but a long, long look, such as is exchanged by lovers; as if all cooks were the kind of person who licks his lips when he sees a pretty girl; as if all male diners were victims of satyriasis, and all female diners nymphomaniacs.

The Meat Epitaph

This is what it was: Sometime in the recent but until now unrecorded past, it was decided by cattle-ranchers that since people were increasingly insistent that "you are what you eat," all cattle on the way to market were to be marked with brief descriptive tags noting the favorite food of each beast, and how much each ate of it. This, it was felt, would both delight the diner and comfort the consumer: people would be able to tell exactly what kind of flavor and texture beef they were purchasing beforehand, and always secure exactly the kind of product most likely to delight their taste (it was something a little like our present-day system of catering to preferences for light and dark meat in chicken). The system set up seemed ideally efficient: first, they attached the tag to each beast on its last day on the ranch, just before the two or three days required for shipment to the slaughterhouse — during which travel time the animal customarily doesn't eat anything, anyway. Once at the slaughterhouse, they carefully removed the tags; and during the slaughtering, duplicated the so-called "parent tag" numerous times, preparing perhaps hundreds of tiny tags for each animal. Directly after, at the packing plant, these were affixed to the proper parts, each section of each animal being separately and appropriately tagged, each as if with an epitaph. But something went wrong with this means of augmenting the diner's delight, and of comforting the consumer. At first, quite predictably, the tags came out reading things like "Much grass, a little moss, medium grain" and "Much grass, much grain, generally ate a lot." And this, as one might expect, proved a great pleasure to the consumer. But then tags began coming through reading things like "A little grass, small grain, many diverse scraps from our table": and "She was our favorite, gave her all we had to give"; and there was one (featured at dinnertime one evening on national television news) saying: "Goodbye, Blackie Lamb, sorry you had to grow up — we'll miss you." Gradually, despite its efficiency, this system somehow ceased to delight the diner, and comfort the consumer. And this is how the practice of the meat epitaph began to become generally neglected during the course of time; and how people came to eat their meat, as they generally do today, partially or wholly blindfolded.

The Taste for All Things Formal

(1) "I ask you: is there one man in the world who doesn't long every now and then for that feeling of formality, that sense of artifice, that certain feeling of neatness and security which only a tuxedo jacket can really provide, surrounding its wearer so snugly with its square-cut shape, its elaborately decorated box-cut cuffs, and above all and before all its glossy, brilliantly shining lapels?" I was lying in bed reading the ads for fancy evening dress, or (as they termed it in the ads beside the social notes column in *The Daily News*) "What every man needs to truly experience that certain feeling of 'stepping out' "; yet still, somehow, I wasn't completely convinced. On the other hand, I did have to admit that I myself that night wished I had a way of experiencing that certain feeling of 'stepping out' instead of lying here like a shut-in, envying the gay formal times people always have in their tuxedos. But then, out of one corner of my eye, I saw it: my brand new armoire. It was true that all it contained were things like buckskin jackets, beads and blue jeans, and tweeds baggy with "that certain lived-in look," all crammed in together and half-falling-off their hangers; but still, there was no mistaking it, the armoire itself was impeccably formal with its tall, rectangular outlines, its elaborate yet symmetrical trim around the sides, and the polished mirrors to the left and right of the center door. So, to achieve that certain feeling of "formally stepping out," I stood up and stepped into the armoire, closing the door after me; and there I spent the entire night having a gay, formal evening. (2) The following morning, while she was dusting around the room, the cleaning lady found me. "What are you doing in there, Sir?" she asked, peering through the keyhole. "Isn't it obvious?—I've been stepping out," I explained. "Did you have a good time, Sir?" she asked enviously, eagerly scan-

ning the interior for noisemakers or perhaps the remnants of a party hat. "Of course I did," I replied; and, anxious to continue to my new-found role of impeccable formal partygoer and general *bon vivant*, I gallantly appended an invitation: "How would you like to come along with me next time?" "Certainly, Sir," she said, "but I have nothing to wear." "Don't worry about that, my dear," I said, gesturing toward the opposite side of the room. (3) And so we began a round of gay formal outings with our first date, stepping out in the finest and most proper manner, me so debonair there in the armoire, she the belle of the ball over there in the corner, wrapped up in my freshly ironed chintz curtains, with the valance pleats folded flat over her face.

Fred, the Neat Pig

(1) Fred was certainly one of the neatest persons you would ever want to meet, and also one of the most polite. In order to keep neat, and not burden you with the sight of any homely or unseemly personal details, he used to put parts of his body that had fallen off back on those portions of his body. For example, whenever a hair fell off his head, he'd pick it up and drop it back on his scalp. If even so much as a beard-strand or an eyelash dislodged, he'd stick it back. If he happened to spit by mistake in the cleanliness of some public place, such as the subway, he'd bend right over and cup it up and put it right back where it belonged. . . . On hot days he'd wrap himself up especially neatly, to prevent the escape of sweat! Fred would glue scabs back on; reattach warts and corns; if he felt something had fallen from his nose during the course of the day, he'd retrace his steps all night in hopes of being able to restore it. Fred's mornings in the bathroom were the most extraordinary of all! (2) He even saved his ear-wax, in order to make candles, so you could see him at all times and admire his neatness better. Yes, when you saw old Fred coming toward you with his flaming candles, his eye-lashes matted, staggering under the weight of warts, his shoetops not too dim despite the deposit of skin products, his clothes all spotted and stained, with piss and shit all over his tunic, the first thing you'd comment on was Fred's neatness. (3) All those people running off when Fred appeared any place would upset any young man, whose virtues were identical with those of tidiness; and so it upset Fred, too. Particularly since his neatness had originally been intended to increase not decrease his circle of friends! Finally, poor Fred tried to solve his sadness at the way others avoided him by carrying around a funnel for use in pouring the tears back down the ducts.

Fast Asleep; or,
The Continuing Adventures of Fred

(1) His profession was that of a sort of long-distance runner in the field of business; no one could be prouder than he was of being sprightly, but in reality young Fred was never faster than when lying there, outstretched, flat on his back, fast asleep. Toes curled, feet enfolded, doubled over backwards, arms akimbo and breathing slowly, he was last clocked in at a rate which exactly exceeded the clock's ability to clock, and reason's ability to logick. Look, here he comes now — there he goes straight past the judges' stand. And even the judges are smiling! Applauded by all, his fans are close to going crazy, he's going so fast, not even moving a muscle! Bravo Fred! But for Fred this speed seems as if it were a dream. A dream? — Yes, that's it, somewhere in the back of his mind he begins to conceive that it's merely a dream. And that's when he begins to slow down. And, as he begins to wake up, he becomes practically inert; already, one would almost consider hiring him to make a speech on this week's subject of permanent political interest, accept the presidency of the corporation, manoeuver for tenure, or sweep the floor in Howard Johnson's. As the alarm rings, the audience gets angry. "Get the lead out!" someone cries; and it's true, he's practically crawling now as he leaps up to brush his teeth, dresses and combs his hair, breakfasts, grabs his briefcase and runs for the door. Seeing this, some good soul at the track calls for a doctor, but it's too late; now, he dashes out the door, hails a cab, and actually arrives early for work — which, to be precise, is as an efficiency expert for IBM. Now, with a kindly but stricken expression, the track doctor stands over him, puzzled about his sudden attack of comatosity, compounded by vast stupefaction and sloth. Meanwhile, back up in the stands, the judges are all stunned

25

and puzzled. Whatever could have happened to Fred, that promising young intellect and athlete? He started out so well only eight hours ago on his 24-hour circular journey around the track, then all of a sudden, one-third of the way around, just as he reached the stands, he dropped out of sight. The judges desert the track, sadly scratching their heads. Now the stands sit there, empty. Silence. (2) Finally, sixteen hours later, around midnight, Fred reappears! He's off in the distance, coming around a curve in the track, slowly but surely crawling along on all fours! As he comes closer we can see big dark circles around his eyes; besides that, he's gibbering nonsense: incorrect mathematical formulae, out-of-date railroad timetables, and such. His mind is obviously exhausted from the business of the day, and now he's giving up all trying, oh, yes, he's giving up all hope, therefore there's hope for him yet; he's forgetting his being asleep is a dream, he's on his feet again, he imagines the crowd is roaring, he remembers the way to fly, the judges and fans come back en masse, now he's really on his way!

A Bad Shoulder

Shivers of splinters run up and down my arm, like sprinters. "Where are they all off to in such a hurry?" I ask my doctor. "They will stop just short of a corneal transplant," he predicts, rustling my recovery chart like a racing form.

A Face in the Trash

(1) I took the top off the trash can outside my bachelor apartment and what should I see there amidst the usual beer cans, peanut shells and fat scraps; citrus-fruit rinds and old poetry textbooks, and the many other anonymous and almost unidentifiable slimes such pails are apt to contain, but a woman's face made entirely out of garbage. And all at once, she smiled at me! — Or were those teeth just a series of overly alive-looking old olive pits? But believe me, everything was perfectly under control. Yes, when our gossipy and scandal-mongering neighbors saw me, lid in hand, leaning over yesterday's garbage, transfixed and looking as if I were about to fall in, everything was perfectly under control, because everything was still perfectly above board between us. (2) But then, as it always does, it happened. Suddenly the woman of my dreams started becoming "forward," began leering instead of smiling, hinting the usual things about "A quick smooch where nobody else can see," her suggestive manner obviously calling for the all-too-usual "fast little visit to my place, baby." But still, everything remained perfectly under control because, to show how firmly I rejected her indecent proposals, I said goodnight and slammed the door to her apartment right smack in her face! (3) Tomorrow, of course, just for the sake of decency and politeness, I'll make it up to her: I'll do it by composing a long note of apology, crumpling it up, and throwing it away just as soon as I finish writing it. Then I'll make it up to her some more by phoning the florist's and ordering a dozen roses to be delivered directly to the garbage pail outside my home. (4) Then I'll really be able to feel once more that things are still rational and perfectly under control, just as perfectly under control as ever.

Respecting Her

I really do respect her, no matter what you might think. How we arrived at this ideal stage in any relationship: It was another typical day in the lover's bower of bliss, she was carving an X in my chest with a steak knife, I was just putting the knitting needles up her anus. Then all at once she turned to me (tightening the ropes around her thighs so that she resembled the kind of trussed-up roast beef Grandmother used to make for a special treat on Sunday); and she hissed through her clenched teeth, "Are you sure you're respecting me enough!" "Respect you enough, respect you enough?" I said, getting to my feet with the aid of crutches and a cane, "respect you enough, of course I respect you enough — but if I don't seem to respect you enough, I'll have to set aside some time soon to respect you enough!" Then I pulled the blindfold back on, and fell onto the floor; and she reached once more for the thumbscrews. But despite this, it was clear that this particular question had drained the joy from our innocent entertainment. And yet the question had seemed so proper at first! And so you see me here now, the wounds beneath these bandages painfully healing, sitting here and writing, scratching with a pencil stub on this miserable piece of rag paper; and what I'm doing here, in case you were wondering, what I'm doing here sitting here with my head in my hands (and this is the proper way to do it, too), is respecting her.

The Nipplewhip

Besides, what else could this be, this toothpick with the long eyelash attached to it with a spot of glue? And, oh, here come the fervent horsemen riding down from the shoulders now, in order to lift up the T-shirt or brassiere. Devils, torturers, these fiends know all too well that too much talk about the nipplewhip could some day cost the poet a fellowship! The poet and his/her love poems sink together into a gloom of handkissing. Meanwhile, at this very moment, all over that part of town with no taste, and no art, laughing people are flinging themselves directly into the path of the nipplewhip.

An Uncooperative Body

(1) After a party during which he consumed 3 martinis, 7 cups of wine, and 4 buckets of beer with several cannisters of cookies baked with hash, he spent the night apologizing to his body by lying around, trying to be nice to it. He attempted to convince it to go to sleep; it needed rest to kill the pain. But it would not listen, and kept awake all the while, aching and throwing up. And, in one spot where he caught his wrist on a doorknob, bleeding a bit. No, his body simply would not forgive him. So, in his drunken delirium, he tried to bribe it to become better; lying down, he threw money all over its chest. Then he offered it (with appropriately courtly gestures) a carton of candy, a box of pornography, and a needle to kill the pain. He even threatened to drag it into the

dark alley behind his alley and beat it up if it didn't get better soon—but at that one, it just smiled back at him a bit sadly. When he saw that, finally, he ended up in a cellar shouting to it for help. (2) Nor did he ever recover. He spent the rest of his life begging to it. At night he whispered into his pillow so as not to wake his wife. A large part of each day was spent in his closet. (3) Finally, he chose poetry as his means of communication.

The Doorway of Perception

If it was one thing he knew—almost automatically—it was that the problem had to be solved, the doorway of perception opened, behind which he was trapped in the parlor of mimicry. So, he knocked on the door. No one opened it. He tried the knob, but it seemed to be stuck. He bent down and attempted to pick the lock using the keys from his own apartment door: no good. Angrily, he arose, walked back across the room, and threw all his weight against it from fifteen feet away! . . . Time after time nothing happened, except that the last time he threw his weight against the door, the entire building fell down around it. Still, the door stood. But this gave him room to run at the door from a still greater distance slowly, he backed up a hundred yards, he launched himself at the door and this time smashed his spinal column. Finally, from his wheelchair, he tried nuclear dynamite. The earth fell down around the door; he realized the sky was falling; he had actually moved both heaven and earth. Just before they fell, he managed to peer at eye level from his

wheelchair through the keyhole. But all he saw was some-
one back there holding up a small, cheap hand-mirror, the
kind they sell at dime-stores; and, in the center of the mirror,
directly opposite the keyhole, looking back at him, was an
eye.

The Mind Friend

Some nights I can almost feel the textures of my moods, so
that even the most modest presence of mind is almost like
having another person lying here next to me. I can nearly
feel her knees beneath me now, just sitting alone here, think-
ing. And as I think on, details of our relationship begin to
return, details such as where first we encountered, how
lovely she was, and what our initial conversations were. I re-
member: it happened about ten years ago, at a literary party.
It is so crowded, I cannot see her face at first; but I recognize
by the circle of festive people she is surrounded by that she
must be either a wonderful conversationalist or some other
kind of attractive or appealing person. Still, it is a shock
seeing her for the first time; and imagine my delight when,
after a few hours of stunned staring at her at a distance, ev-
erybody else has left, and we find ourselves alone at last in a
corner. And imagine my surprise when after a brief dialogue
I take the hand of the mind and offer to take her home in a
taxicab; and she accepts. What a reasonable creature! In the
taxicab I pat her knee, to make sure this feeling is real; and to
make sure that I am real to her; and sure enough, it's true —
she doesn't move! The taxicab pulls up in front of her door,

31

which happens to be in a familiar building in my very own district; at her front door, which happens to be the same as mine, she invites me up for coffee and a night-cap. Upstairs among friendly surroundings again, she becomes still more open with me; we chat for a while, and reach the next stage of our intimacy; I help her loosen a stuck window and finally fix an ancient leak beneath the sink. She feels at home; it's dawn by then. She invites me to sit down and relax; and she surprises me by taking out a forgotten guitar from underneath the bed and singing some songs. They are all bittersweet, idealistic songs which it is plain to see are all about herself . . . about things like her loneliness, her disappointment in various people, her isolation, her lack of real company in this distant city. . . . By then, it's obviously time to leave. But I ask her if we can make a specific appointment to meet again soon, perhaps the very next day, and she agrees; but even though we do, I know that the next time I try to make contact with this particular mind, her guitar will be gone again, she will be gone, and I will have truly lost her. . . .

II. Midnight at The Hotel Hell

Midnight at The Hotel Hell

Midnight at The Hotel Hell. It's hard to see in this darkness, it's hard to read, it's hard to do anything. The walls are so thin everybody else would hear, and learn just what you are doing, just exactly what evil act. So you extract your penis from the hole for razor-blade rejection in the bathroom, and you come out into the bedroom, brush aside the giant plastic doll with the "unusual accessories every man is literally sure to adore," sit down on the edge of the bed and begin whispering nice things about the neighbors, in the hope that they will lose the desire you are sure they certainly have to kick down these walls or bash down the cardboard door and otherwise break in and kill you.

*

This hotel is full of elderly gentlemen so old that when they ask one of the bellhops to get them a woman, and give him a five-dollar tip, all that is expected is that he will place an anonymous obscene phone call in their name. But whom do the bellhops dial? It's always a certain Suzy, who writes the "social notes" column for a famous underground newspaper. Suzy is a fat or thin, disagreeable, knock-kneed quadruple amputee unpleasant lesbian, but everybody in this particular hotel thinks it's "nice" that she takes an interest in sex, and particularly in you: and of course, you have to agree. "But why is she so fat?" you hear yourself asking yourself. "Because, as a journalist, she's always gathering new material," you hear yourself reply, hoping nobody else heard. Later on, for the same five dollars, the same old men get the right to masturbate by leaving the needle-point shower on full force. They can also use the falling water to kill mosquitoes and drown the cockroaches.

35

At the service desk: A bellhop dressed in a bright red uni-
form is shouting "Call for Philip Mor-aze, call for Philip
Mor-aze!" Mr. Morris appears, and twenty other bellhops
dressed in bright red jump out from in back of the message
desk and begin beating him up, ending up by twisting a knife
up his nose, and disordering his formal clothes. "Too bad
this man was so deaf," the manager explains, "so that he
couldn't hear that what Johnny, our jolly head message-desk
bellhop was saying, was not "Call for Philip Morris," but
rather "That's all for Philip Morris." "I would have made the
same mistake myself," you are about to freely confess; but
then you catch yourself in time. Then you notice a mistake
in communication you really did make: the hotel's slogan on
the prospectus which initially convinced you to check in
here never really did read "Ready to serve, seventeen effi-
cient bellhops," but rather "Ready to be served, seventeen
efficient bellyhopes."

*

Hungry suddenly, you notice a sign in the gracious old
lobby: "You Eat Well at The Hotel Hell: Food to Feed The
Whole Man!" It's a bit menacing, that slogan; but still, it just
might turn out to be the ideal restaurant! So you take the ele-
vator down to the dining-room, which you've heard for some
reason has been located on the lowermost floor of all. But
after you get off the elevator in the sub-sub-basement, you
notice it keeps going down. Something is wrong with the
dining-room, too; it seems that the grand old relic of great
days located in the sub-sub-basement has been converted
somewhat; now it's a self-service cafeteria. And even as a
self-service cafeteria, you notice at once it has several draw-

36

backs: while only one course is available, drinking of any kind is prohibited; and there is a waiter to tip, who also doubles as a wine waitress. And he lets you know at once by the usual well-known waiter's ways that you are there simply for the purpose of providing sufficient tips. A friendly old man in a top hat leans over and begins a conversation to help pass the time while you are waiting for your waiter. "That waiter," he remarks, "has what my dear old friend Suzy calls 'the typical American guttersnipe servant's idea of good service' "; but then, before he can finish his sentence, he suddenly falls off his chair, after receiving a chop, a karate chop from the waiter, who was standing there motionless behind you all this time, waiting for just such a remark. "But what is a guttersnipe?" you find yourself wondering. And so, all through dinner — even as the waiter is breathing down your neck to get you to dine faster so that another party may sit down in order to tip — and so as not shock the other patrons with your insensitivity — you have to sit there over your meal, staring and unable to eat a thing, as if shocked into immobility by the insulting phrase the man in the top hat reported was uttered by anti-social Suzy; and also you have to generate some sympathy and understanding for poor misguided Suzy and show it seriously in your eyes; and finally you must look down as if mortified by this vision you know you are expected to entertain, this vision of some poor snipe, sloshing around among the dank gutters, sewers and top hats of soul-destroying Capitalism.

*

"Food for the Whole Man" — and, in fact, you begin dinner with knucklebone soup, with toes for hors d'oeuvres and fingers for toothpicks; some glandular oysters are followed by a

37

torso steak, garnished with a little hair with brain still cling-
ing to it on the side. The "seconds" are overly generous:
Limbs, limbs of all kinds, arms under glass, legs glacé, mem-
bers still faintly moving. By the time you finish eating at the
restaurant at the Hotel Hell, you haven't so much dined in
style as given a corpse a complete physical examination.
Meanwhile, back in the kitchen, the cook is waiting for you
with a carving knife, furious that you haven't yet sent your
compliments to the chef for so skilfully preparing so elabo-
rate a feast. You belch; someone announces in a formal voice
that the autopsy is over; and instead of the waiters for whom
you have have come to feel such great sympathy during the
time you've been here, four pallbearers enter and carry the
remains of the dinner out the door.

*

The great sign! The great sign! They've changed the great
sign outside the restaurant. It doesn't read "You Eat Well at
The Hotel Hell," it reads "You Bleed Well at The Hotel
Hell." And sure enough, the next night, as you leave the res-
taurant after another delightful dinner (how quickly you've
learned to appreciate both the food and the service!), you
look around at the lively, animated, excited people at the
other tables and notice that they are all sitting there ex-
pressing themselves with all that deafening enthusiasm with
their arms held out and blood running down over their
wrists and cuffs; and here and there, bowing, smiling waiters
are at work opening up the veins of the new arrivals. Moving
swiftly to the bar for a drink, you wonder exactly why you've
been permitted to escape. You walk down a little ramp, and
enter the bar, where a sign promises "Celebrity Entertain-
ment tonight"; it turns out that your mother is working there
as a topless go-go girl.

The Thermometer and the Future

This cold is awful, how did the temperature get down there so low? It must have slipped down there by sneaking past us, all hunched over, dressed in the black cloak of night. Because this morning, we are shocked to awake to a white world of magic: all the hailstones bouncing, and our spit suspended. It's time now to make a decision which is truly a matter of life and death: whether to leave right now, in search of some other, more congenial climate; or, if we haven't the nerve to leave, whether to solve everything by becoming a snowman, which is to say the kind of man who only grows when it snows.

Tree Surgery

Seated in a tree, we are about to saw off the afflicted member. But where do we begin the incision? If, conservatively, we saw too close to the trunk, we deprive the branch of the possibility of a modest regeneration by means of sprigs. On the other hand, the work of the most efficient and effective tree surgeons has certainly never been signalled by a sprinkling of tons of tiny twigs over the turf. Another factor: before proceeding, it is useful to estimate how many branches will need to be removed, since in some cases so many branches would have to be subtracted in order to save the tree, that there might be nothing but a trunk left, and the tree would look better and live longer if it were simply left sick. And beyond that, there is one additional consideration: it is necessary, at present, to remember that the principles of good tree-surgery matter little in comparison with the worst danger, and the most frequent medical mistake in the forest — which is that of having sawed off the branch upon which we have been seated, and being in the midst of being deposited

The Landscape in Process

(1) The landscape in process: Its vegetation slowly growing, but also, on the table, there is the carefully prearranged still life on which the realist artist has labored for a good part of his life—only to have a hand reach down and seize the apples, with all their connotations of evil, the grapes, reminding one of bacchanalia, and then the pears, pointed like ladies. Then the hand lifts them up and begins to eat them all! So, perhaps this arm must be the ultimate artist? Other examples of artistic progress hereabouts: the view from my window of the windows opposite, with the figures moving in them; with the brown window frames crumbling away, and which the landlord-artist has finally painted grey. And then there is my role in all this art: my myopia gradually growing worse, and my eyeglasses gradually becoming too weak to correct it; my typewriter ribbon dimming as I type; the atoms of this chair bringing it nearer to its version of universal esthetic Apocalypse, when it will collapse and dump this realist artist onto the floor. (2) Thus we can see that for the complete realist, this entire landscape must be a work of art; only your poetry, O masters of memorized metrics and measured metaphor, only your poetry, O masters of manufactured emotion, deprives me of the sense of the presence of art; and of the pleasures of vision and change.

The Melancholy Moralist

Am I really supposed to stay here with the rest of these people making the usual surreptitious motions, tentative gestures, and shifting around guiltily from foot to foot? Because I can feel that there is obviously not going to be enough room to move in this room. To scratch the top of my head I have to go slipping my arm around the side of my head in a guilty way, as if it were a journey by Rolls-Royce around a bend in a mountain road in the poverty region, all the while praying that nobody accuses the hollow of my armpit of causing competition with a shut-down coal mine. Just so, I am amply assured that whenever I reach up to scratch my nose, a boxcar falls over in Alabama, as does a beer can in the Alhambra. And should I lower my eyelashes to express the requisite embarrassment, a bird's nest falls out of the tree in a field beside the farm. According to these definitions, I'll have to black out both my eyes in order to be able to say I see! And if I decide to deeply inhale, the tender finger of the saintly child beside me here, the one giving me the long lecture on delicacy, holding me by the lapel with one hand, and poking me in the chest with the other, becomes blunted. Also, inhaling risks bursting the stained glass windows in this beautiful room they have locked us all in. The Poetry Library would fall! The orphanage be eaten up by an ogre! And to think, I originally came here to this place because I heard it was the ideal place to go if you wanted to open a career in modern dance.

The Disappointed Philanthrophist

How do you feel, you who yearned half your life for endless friends, but discover that all you've ended up with is a succession of clever operators? Well-schooled in charitable ways at only the most priviledged of academies, how could you have realized that when you said your first friendly hello to any stranger, your voice would inevitably be tape-recorded, the sound amplified and stored away for eventual use in shattering eggshells among the indigent egg-suckers of Peru; that during any appearance in public the slightest stray breeze of your celebrated sympathetic breath would be compressed for use in running a waterwheel set up horizontally by some local government idiot in the very midst of the provinces of Sand; that should you even go so far as to smile your gold-toothed smile at a passing stranger, the second time around he was apt to return with a jewelry-appraiser disguised as a desert saint; or that when you held out your hand to the professional beggar, he would invariably place it palm down on a butcher's scale? Oh, so very well-trained in the care and feeding of all the would-be recipients of anything they can lay their hands on whatsoever, how did you feel the first time you noticed that, since you were said to weep so often with concern, the back door of your modest home had become completely surrounded by a series of secret souvenir stands selling tears?

Xmas Lights

The Christmas lights are on again on the roof of the building across the street. Twenty-two bulbs, shaped like a tree! Once a year the lights of charity go up, reminding you of the end of yet another year; once again the lights of generosity mark the time, literally bringing you a certain amount closer to your death.

Errors of the Magi

Here come the Magi again . . . there aren't too many this time, though . . . and this time, the Magi are wearing duncecaps. 1 plus 3 equals 7? 2 plus 2 equals 8? No, nothing like that. They didn't make that kind of mistake. This time, the mistake they made was to try to increase their popularity by going around wearing duncecaps as a sign of both their humanity and humility. That way, they hoped, they would both reach a broad general public, and satisfy everybody. And — instead of acknowledging the fresh applause with delight — they even went so far as to hang their heads, as if in remembrance of their former pride. So their fame grew and grew. However, from bending down so often that way, one day their duncecaps fell off, bouncing down the untold number of stairs beneath their well-known golden thrones. And, there at the very bottom, awaits the predictable mob of half-wits. And the half-wits snatch up the duncecaps, slice off the tips with their ever-present switchblades, and use the

duncecaps as megaphones through which to further remind
the Magi of their future and former shortcomings. Or, to hit
them with. The Magi slump over, limp in their thrones.
Now, today, several even wish they had not pretended to be
even still less intelligent than they actually were.

The Cultural Lovers

(1) To celebrate many long, long years of cultural relation-
ship, and their mutual belief that the main function of litera-
ture and other culture is to bring whole peoples of the world
into closer and more understanding contact, they had an-
other dinner together. But before dinner, they exchanged
anniversary gifts in suitable celebration of their liberal world-
view: She gave him a lovely set of uranium cufflinks pictur-
ing Albert Schweitzer at the piano; he returned the favor
with a beautiful Mahatma Gandhi moneyclip. The dinner
she prepared was the kind they invariably found tasteful as
well as nourishing. They began the evening's festivities with
a series of hors d'oeuvres from a recipe book which, being a
literary person, she had just published: "The Desert Saint
Cookbook"; then followed that with their favorite private
culinary improvisation, a rare steak shaped just like the head
of I. A. Rodale, respected authority on vegetarianism; and a
cabbage, in the form of William Shakespeare's face. And all
this was consumed using their special celebrative silver-
ware: the cocktail forks, cheese-knives and dessert-spoons
consisting of replicas of the many starving but by now unfor-

tunately deceased children they loved so much to discuss during their many long years together; and the larger serving pieces, the forks and knives, in the shapes of children whose growth had merely been stunted by malnutrition. Clash!— For the thirteenth time that night they toasted with their champagne glasses especially manufactured for them as a thank-you for a substantial donation to Alcoholics Anonymous, Inc. Finally, a bit tipsy over dessert, but ectastic that art had finally been made to serve real people and human need, just like all the most serious and celebrated TV comedians said it should, they threw their dessert glasses into the roaring fireplace, all the while praising the bracing rigors of Soviet winters, especially in Siberia. Then they fell asleep on top of each other, like the innocent babes they knew they were. (2) That night, their sleep was disturbed. An atomic bomb in the shape of a peace dove went off; war was declared by a peace-loving President, and as the dying millions went streaming past on stretchers, the cultural lovers dreamt simultaneously that they had perished in a suicide pact, by laughing themselves to death at a group "sensitivity session" held in a local gymnasium.

Two Figures Clutching Each Other

Two figures are in a field locked together, impressive, digni-
fied, against the moonlight, just like giants . . . No, that's
wrong, actually they're only the neighbors from the two
next-door estates, the formal places with the big houses with
columns, where all the unofficial nationless diplomats live;
and what is going on is a strange combination of embracing
and assaulting. The struggle has been going on since sun-
down, and the end of the perfect cocktail party; this long
snakelike coil has been wrapped for hours around them
both . . . Is it then perhaps Laocoön? No, it's a garden hose
one person is trying to choke the other with, to convince the
other of his good intentions toward him. The cries of protes-
tation grow so terrible, that here in my backyard, beside the
brick barbeque, I bump my bottle of beer into my bad-behav-
ing big-bosomed beloved; and she, my bad-behaving big-bo-
somed beloved, laughs, flicks some wine back in my eye;
and we both laugh. We misbehave that way—and worse—
until, in the midst of all the shouts and scuffling, the crack-
ling fingers bent back and the plucking out of hair from next
door, you can't help but hear what the silhouettes are saying;
and we stop misbehaving. "No, please, please," one is plead-
ing, "Please believe me; I'm glad you rang me up after six
months the other day; but please believe me: it's an incred-
ible coincidence, because just before you phoned me to in-
vite me over here this afternoon I was going to phone you to
invite you to my house!" "I beg your pardon," the other in-
sists, "it's an incredible coincidence, but even before I
phoned to invite you over I phoned you previously only I got
a busy signal; and what I was actually planning to do was
not only invite you over for a drink, but also for an entire
weekend!" "No, no, I'm the one you have to forgive!" the
other cries out, "because just before you called to invite me

49

over to your place I was just reaching for the phone to invite you out to my summer lodge for a weekend of waterskiing and polo; but unfortunately your call came and prevented me from doing so. What a terrible disappointment I had to pick up the receiver and actually speak with you!" "Oh, I'm so sorry that happened, too!" the other exclaims, "because just before you reached me I was about to telegraph you to ask you to become a permanent member of my household, share my wife with me, and turn over my bank-book to you—except that you keep on complicating our relationship so by talking to me!" "Oh, what a coincidence!" the other silhouette shrieks back, "Now you've gone and done it, I'm so sorry you said that, because just as soon as I got home I was going to send you several smoke-signals confessing to you that I realized not long ago that you've always been my long-lost true love; so you can imagine how disappointed I was to see you today, I was looking forward to communicating with you so much..." At that point, clutching each other tighter than ever, the two struggling figures disappear out of earshot. The next morning, after the best night in bed we have ever had, my bad-behaving big-bosomed beloved and I wake, walk across the lawn, and find the two fast friends lying there in a ditch behind a hedge, arms still around each others' necks, eyes popping out of their heads, strangled. The autopsy was terse but suitably discreet: it explained that they had died of politeness.

Arch Poem

I must tell you, I tell my aristocratic friend Philip, my foot arch aches today. Philip raises his eyelashes; he's known, since he heard it as a child, that to complain about illness lacks style, it places an unfair burden on the interlocutor. So I change my tack, making light of my pain. "Ah yes, arch, arch, everything is so arch, I see you're even arching your eyebrows over there; tell me now, Philip, does that hurt you?" I can tell that Philip likes that, because as if to make amends, and to show his appreciation for the tremendous stylishness I have just revealed, he goes so far as to ask me how I hurt my foot. Also, he goes so far as to ask me if it "really hurts." "No, no," I realize I have to cry out, "now that we've begun speaking about arches I've forgotten about all that, all I can think about now are how many triumphal arches there are scattered along the highways and byways of the body, and about the expanses that lie between them, making it difficult for the average casually inspecting tourist to scan them with just a glance; or even for the lover to do so, traveling along on the wings of a kiss. Ah, just think, Philip, isn't the entire body a variety of arch, with crotch as keystone while the buttresses are arms?" By this time Philip is beside himself, delirious to have a friend as aristocratically detached from personal adversity as me; and the next thing I know, he's down on his knees, imploring me to tell him everything about my foot, my body, my entire health. Indeed, eventually he actually swoons with delight over my witty company, so that I have to go off to get him a bottle of smelling salts, limping and hopping on my bad foot to the doctor.

51

The Allegorical Figure of Compulsory Melancholy or, The Midget-Pervert-Quadruple-Minority-Group-Amputee

(1) The allegorical figure of compulsory melancholy is being wheeled into the party again. Happily, the hostess is smiling even more than before; and at least it is appearing as late as possible. Still, it is here: The celebrated Midget-Pervert-Quadruple-Minority-Group-Amputee, set upon a little cart: and behind this cart, on a trailer for the sake of neatness, is a tray bringing together all its missing arms and legs, all tied up tightly into sailor's knots. (2) And of course, when it makes its entrance at this party where a genuine celebration of something seemed to be going on, the bacchantes suddenly cease, setting down their wine glasses after calling for plastic coasters from the servants they always announce they are just about to abolish; you can hear little flipping sounds as even the most blissful orgiasts drop both bosoms and bottoms with a general guilty look; and over in one corner, an upright flower set beside a card saying it is a subtle symbol for your cock, falls over. (3) The conversation grows more careful now; now, no one dares balance his cup of nectar on his head so as to gesture with greater enthusiasm with his arms in the air; now, no one even dares seek a decent warmth by embracing his nearest neighbor. (4) This of course is one of those parties where, as you are about to leave, the hostess appears at the door with an axe held like some sort of barrier across the lap of her chiffon gown, and tells you she is so worried about whether you had a good time. (5) And of course, you have to reassure her, for two reasons: (a) because obviously the last person who failed to make a graceful exit at the last party became the Midget-Pervert-Quadruple-Minority-Group-Amputee at this party, and (b) because this way also, you will have the luxury of being invited back next time to what is, after all, just about the only series of celebrations given in our particular area.

The Ancient and Elevating Art of Urine Retention

In the dead man's hospital room, I, the nightwatchman, the part-time poet and proverbial self-seeking time-serving civil-service worker on the side, find the remains of the recently deceased: a ragged and torn old notebook surrounded by 57 bedpans full of water and thinned blood. What could have happened here? To help kill the time until morning, we open the notebook, select a passage at random, and begin to read from the dead man's work. Even though it is not in verse, still, we can tell that this particular patient appears to have had his problems! The passage reads: "From this room I am in, a terrible scream: my roommate, an old man, had been practising what he identified in a whisper, before the nurses came, as 'The Ancient and Elevating Art of Urine Retention'; and now, beside the bed, three naked nurses dressed in the accoutrements of storm-troopers are trying to 'get a little something' out of him. 'It's mine, it's mine, so let me have it, so let me have it!' the old man keeps on crying; and, unfortunately, those three naked nurses are taking him all too literally. . . . After several hours of this, finally there is an interruption; someone from the American Medical Association arrives, and explains to the old man's corpse that the nurses were only doing their duty; then a socialworker appears and explains that the experiment was undertaken for reasons of the public good, and accuses the old dead man with mouth still frozen in the position of screaming of the worst kind of self-centeredness, selfishness, and greed; then, after they carry my poor old roommate out, they begin to turn to me . . ." And that's where the diary breaks off! Immediately I begin to shout words of sympathy for both the patient and his one-time roommate; this nightwatchman, part-time poet and proverbial self-seeking time-serving civil-service worker finally begins to cry out down the halls for justice and revenge. . . . but that's when the buzzer goes off, the buzzer that sounds to signify the new day and the coming dawn; — and, therefore, time to go home. How time flies, when you have a way of killing it! And so I hurry off, not only because as nightwatchman I am obviously not responsible for anything in the daytime, but also because by not pushing this thing too far I hope to maintain the sympathy of the hospital administration, so as to rise to the next highest position in this particular establishment: that of Brain Surgeon.

Two Notes from the Acme Health Farm

I. Acupuncture

A tiny needle needs to be placed athwart the neck; a skilled surgeon hired from an ancient civilization. So with our penchant for mail-order panaceas we send out our letters from our tasteful, quasi-literary treat at the Acme Health farm and count the moments until, as promised, halfway around the world, a surgeon gets on a ship. Who is he? For acupuncture, we expect a man of gentle yet general culture, with a long white beard dragging along behind him as he walks, like a rag rug. But at quayside we are surprised when a talkative, quasi-Mongoloid starts coming down the gangplank, with a burning eye, a hammer, and a handshake full of nails, telling us all what's good for us. Is he an imposter? We health-adventurers eye one another in suspicion and puzzlement — but doubt not that we retain the most delicate demeanor withal!

II. Sturgery

When we get enough mental problems invulnerable to both psychotherapy and chemotherapy, we write the International Intellectual Medical Arts Talent Pool for a skilled surgeon. The next week, a tank arrives with a fish in it, leaping in and out of a hoop and giving hand-signals with his tail. Attached is a tag: a note on it says: "Here's your skilled sturgeon, hope you enjoy him." The sturgeon successfully performs seven successful lobotomies before somebody we consider obviously some disgusting right-wing type finally discovers the error.

55

Rabblehorn

(1) Go ahead, lift the rabblehorn, trumpet. It's a long piece of tubing, covered with brass and aluminum fittings tied up into love knots looking like little cat's cradles. You carry it over your shoulder with the vortex of the horn stuck well out in front. Knees high, the true enthusiast will practically prance to the applause. Obviously, almost everybody must approve of the sound of the rabblehorn, because they've all heard its sentiments before. (2) Your only enemy is a very large frog. He sits there in the middle of the roadway looking tremendous and green. I put him there. (3) And when you come around the bend in the road with your entire entourage, every last person cheering, he opens his mouth and you march in. He continues sitting there, while you wander around inside, and while the rabblehorn goes on playing its confident tune. Only it's sad now, and a bit muffled. . . . (4) No! — That kind of wistful vulnerability in this picture is all too expected, all too acceptable — that's not what happened at all! What happens in reality is that I unwind all forty feet of the rabblehorn, you blabbermouth, I take it and stuff it up your fat ass. It seems to hurt. In fact, what am I saying, it does hurt.

The Muse in Armor

Who is that over there urging us to remain ever-open to experience, ever-vulnerable, even to the would-be obliterators of our lives, and everything we know to be so? As soon as we open our eyes, we get a full-length view of him/her/it: a crouching figure, completely encased in a suit of armor. Also, as this figure lectures on, we can see that it has more teeth than we have ever seen in the mouth of any other previous person. But when we try and tell this figure things like life has not been too kind to us lately, or even that we have been bitten too often not to be bitter and that—at the risk of offending its philosophy—we would like to survive somewhat, and that we might even like our poetry to assist in this, it stands up in a huff which is not entirely without a sense of threat and—clanking like a Sherman tank and a Mack truck combined—it stomps out of the room.

The Adventures of Resentment

Resentment, you remember—since somebody told you once—spreads like a stain. But somehow, now it's also a point of light in the brain, a train coming toward you down a long tunnel. It pulls up at the little station and you get on. Out of the tunnel, beyond the station, you ride ten thousand miles. Out in the light you immediately become the world's most celebrated traveler. Little children gather by the railway line to see you pass by. For miles around, the multitude grows grudgingly aware of your integrity. Chugging along, sitting in the window, your tongue out, making faces, and giving everybody The Finger, you become a sight yourself; you grow almost as popular as Lincoln's Coffin. Rounds of applause, stompings of feet at crossroads! Finally, contracts arrive; gifts, grants, awards, offers to appear in public or on educational TV! You even begin to look forward to further adventures. That's exactly when, for some reason, the point of light begins to pull slowly away, back down the track. You find yourself standing in some stupifying station in Idaho with all the home folks, eyes dull, a blank look on your face, loving everything and finally cleansed of resentement.

Variations on Reverence for Life
for D. L.

Certainly we have reverence for life: Open-mouthed we stand before the temple of life; then we throw up. But I remember the old days, when in all innocence I used to stand around outside the temples on tiptoe, listening to the strains of inspiring music. Until one day, when, owing to my long-standing interest in choral singing, I was actually allowed to enter. Still, I must admit, my sentiments were at best second-hand. I became part of the great tradition of the listener in the chorus. Of course, I was allowed to hum some. And it was my true vocation, everybody told me. But it was not. Nor was it even my true avocation. My true avocation was growing avocados. I used to place them in glasses with a little water, and sing to them. And unlike my alleged true avocation, my avocados sprouted, silently climbing in unlikely, irregular, but somehow logical patterns all over the ceilings, roofs, and rafters. Now, when I catch myself standing out in front of the temple of life, gawking, I can stop myself: I've discovered that the most effective way for me to avoid throwing up, is by utterly shutting up. Despite its obvious eloquence, my poetry is probably mainly a way of shutting up.

Living with Adversity

There are some mountains you can't move. Moreover, not only that, but you will find yourself under severe pressure to sit there at their feet, lying around for half your life, like some sweet boy or girl scout, saying how happy you are, and exclaiming about how good it is to simply experience such scenic beauty, and at such great length. After all, haven't you been explicitly notified that generations upon generations of calendar-makers have been literally depending upon these distant romantic views for their support? — so that even if you decide to climb them, you know you shouldn't, since it might throw a great many people out of work! Every step would have to be an apology! Every step a regret! Finally, once they know you know the feelings expected of you — what great guilt — they hand you the spiked hiking shoes. It's kind of these people, you know you're supposed to feel; except that you will notice that instead of being on the outside, of the shoe, facing down, the spikes have been placed on the inside of the shoe, facing up — a simple mistake, you know you will have to hasten to reassure them. That's when you learn that all the local artisans and shoemakers, too, are rumored to be terribly upset about their little error; and so you have to visit their basements to reassure them that you forgive them, too, and to apologize for causing them upset, before you start to climb. Still, slowly, you ascend.

IV. Household Hallucinations

The Voyage of Self-Discovery

It's the voyage of self-discovery: it started out with enormous sails, a drunken Captain, and a bosun going toot-toot. Now, when you think you hear them piping you to quarters, it usually turns out to be a reference to a heavy smoker who is about to receive interest at the bank. So now the ship sits upon this bank, fifteen feet above sea level, dripping ooze from all her portholes. It seems a pleasant enough little bay, however, and the Captain, who has just discovered after the disaster that he is still an incurable optimist, wonders if, given enough time and money, the old hulk might not be converted from a former four-masted schooner to a large barge for inland waterway travel; or even, just possibly, a houseboat.

An Enormous Eartrumpet Was Found Floating Far Out at Sea

(1) The ship is moving away from the dock, all handkerchiefs raised and aflutter. Everyone wishes the newlyweds well, wishes them the finest and most traditional joy they can imagine—"Bon Voyeur! Bon Voyeur!" is what everybody is shouting. Believe it or not, I spent long years of my life believing that "Bon Voyage" was what I was hearing, until I realized what they were actually saying. I rationalized away the shock of recognition by referring back to the nature of wedded bliss itself, since isn't what marriage represents,

essentially, the passionate desire on the part of lovers that their love be made public? And how far is this from the wish that lovers be granted an opportunity to literally make love in public? Surely, if best friends and relatives were really sincere, wouldn't it be only natural for them—although they might not themselves be able to come along on the honeymoon—to wish to send along some sort of surrogate on the voyage? Yes, surely: to wish that lovers be skilfully spied upon through keyholes, transoms, or even face-to-face is the only decent thing to wish for at such a time! Only a fiend would wish the lovers the obvious alternative to a "Bon Voyeur"—i.e., a "Mauvais Voyeur." What would that be a wish for, anyway?—a person who keeps hanging around the lovers' bower of bliss all the time, yet who keeps on congenitally objecting to, or else missing things? A Peeping Tom in a blindfold? A blind man with a perversion? (2) Thanks to this clear-sighted logic, I have gradually come to grasp the deepest meaning of the institution of marriage, not to mention the situation down here at the docks. For a while, for the first time (as I am sure you can see) I even felt in tune with reality, and normalcy, generally. (3) But then, nasty news: I received word that I was somehow indulging once again in error and illusion. The word came in a plain brown envelope, too, when somebody sent me an enormous, old-fashioned eartrumpet. So now the truth is resoundingly out: there are clearly some people who feel that I ought to take corrective action; and that what I obviously ought to do, as the only possible corrective solution, instead of going around fantasizing, mishearing and misunderstanding everything, is get myself a wife. (4) True, I hear that this new life of mine would be only a modest beginning—that it begins by merely making one's existence somewhat duller down here at the docks. Still, the possibilities, I understand, are endless. . . . But after all, wouldn't this new life be better than going around as I do, imagining that life, despite its conventional surfaces, may really be subtle, sly, exotic and exciting as a whisper? Yes: I ask you: wouldn't life really be better this new way, as some people say? Really now — wouldn't it? Eh? Pardon me? What say?

The Detective Wife

Really, I guess, the marriage ceremony was where I first should have become somewhat suspicious about the direction our relationship was taking — really, perhaps, I should have realized *something* when she appeared at the wedding in a bridal outfit consisting of a sword-cane, a black cape, checked knickers, a Sherlock Holmes cap, and an old, fuming meerschaum pipe! And what kind of a groom's outfit was this the bride's family had ordered for me to wear? — a brand new convict's uniform, with my social-security number inscribed across the chest and my date of birth in large letters across the back! Also, perhaps I should have become a bit more concerned when we began to go out to parties at which she had heard other attactive ladies might be present, and she made her entrance bent over double, nose pressed to the floor, sniffing. Oh, she was the only guest whom other guests would greet by immediately turning their faces to the wall and all their pockets inside out! No, she was no mere amateur! Never out of practice, in the country she could detect the presence of moonshine liquor in a solid gold flask in a tree trunk at a distance of fifty feet; in the city, the possession of illegally imported tax-free cigarettes of some kind in the trouser cuffs of nearly every passing stranger. And as for passing through her eyes in a fit of passion, it was like clearing Cuban-American customs! But still, I probably wouldn't have suspected something had gone wrong with our intimate interpersonal relationship until one night, just as we were turning in, and despite my tendency not to pry too deeply, I finally got up the nerve to ask her just who that person was who kept on slipping into bed with us every evening as soon as I began to drift off to sleep; and she thought she explained everything by answering: "Elementary, my dear fellow, that's Doctor Watson." And to think how innocently this all began; and how flattered I was when I first began to experience that feeling familiar to so many husbands and lovers: that of being a desperately wanted man.

Discouraging Evening

Hiccupping sounds in the night — then pretty soon the smell of cat vomit beneath the bed where my life's companion and I are lying. One of us ought to get up and clean it up, but both of us are pretending not to hear. Neither of us moves even when the odor suffuses the air. And it's not that we were up much late last night, it's not that we've been fucking; we haven't been anything, much. It's just that we're both too plain lazy to move. Also, the thing is that we really can't get too upset about the cat vomiting, we're so sick of ourselves, and each other. We tuck our two heads under our arms and under our two pillows and await shit to fall from the ceiling, anything.

"Bed Tablets"

I had been noticing that my sleeping quarters were beginning to look a little shabby lately, so that it was quite a relief when I went to the medicine cabinet and the label on a little bottle of white pills caught my eye. It was marked "Bed Tablets." So, to begin to neaten up the room, I went back to the bedroom and sprinkled Bed Tablets all over my cot and went to sleep on the floor, to allow the room time to recover. And sure enough, the next morning, I noticed a great improvement in the room — in any case, my bed was certainly beginning to look a whole lot better to me! So, lately I've been wondering whether — no questions asked of course — my doctor might be willing to write me out a prescription for "Wall Cream."

The Pills

Midnight: its hidden significance: all over the city a million of the sleeping pills people are supposed to take one hour before bedtime are starting to dissolve in five hundred thousand stomachs. Now, at last, absolutely without sentimentality, we are truly part of a world of brothers beneath the skin.

*

He tossed and turned so that when he tried to catch up on lost sleep in the late afternoon, just before dinnertime, his wife used to secretly affix a salad bowl to his backbone, as he lay there. Russian dressing was his specialty.

*

We use the phrase "going to sleep" because sleep really is a place to go to; we spend all day arriving there, driving hard down the highways of staying awake, under the underpasses and across the shortcuts; and we have to travel far, speeding through all of time at the rate of 16 hours per day.

*

Looking for cool places on a pillow on a summer night—No Columbus ever set out on a more difficult mission, or a more perilous one, we have come to recognize; consider our fate, for example, lying here completely upsidedown, having fallen out of bed, with our feet in the air.

The Pills and the Water

To get some rest, finally, I dropped the pills out of the mouth of the little bottle and onto the palm of my hand; then I flipped them toward my open mouth. Imagine my surprise when the pills went straight over my shoulder and onto the bathroom floor! So, to be consistent, and also to make sure that everything remained orderly, and that I had taken the pills properly, I flipped some water over my shoulder after them, also onto the floor.

The Awards of Water

At first it seemed as if it were the morning coffee again, overflowing in the percolator with the usual loud hiss; but then, when I reached the kitchen, I saw that the brown stain on the white stove was in the form of a "splash," which is to say a circle with fringed edges; and that it was actually only another form of water setting its seal of approval on solids. Do raindrops act any differently, I wondered; do they approve, too, with their pure, glueless, transparent stickers? Even now, as the morning coffee is brewing, we can be sure that the dew is descending in all directions to award billions of blue ribbons to everything firm; that the rushing of rivers is like the roar of applause; and that the only reason why we do not regard the Pacific Ocean as absolutely solid rock is that it is obviously much too much like an auditorium full of people cheering and stamping feet.

Evaporation

Mid-morning: the sun is evaporating everything everywhere again. The amazing thing about the sun is not its brightness but its thoroughness; although its rate of evaporation may vary, nonetheless it keeps on operating everywhere. From what direction, on this sunny, sparkling morning, isn't water being pumped? We can see that the sun absorbs the dampness from every sandy surface, but also it lifts up a manhole cover and slowly sneaks water out from under it, too, finishing its drink by sucking greedily at the rim. A leaf covers a wet spot about the size and shape of a small coin, but then the wind blows, and the sun comes and slips it back into its back pocket. And afterwards, carefree, burping all day long, it goes off, whistling, down the afternoon sky. Nor is there any exception to this either. Imagine that underneath some man's shoe is some pure, fresh water that escaped and that a man decides to be stubborn and keep. The man waits for the sun to drop back beneath the horizon of dryness. But Mankind is standing in a drain. Even on days when it doesn't rain, what man doesn't inhabit a toilet?

Dress Soup

We run out of laundry pails so, one morning, before she goes away for the day, my rushed beloved uses one of the extra cooking pans standing on the stove to soak her dress in. Then, during the late afternoon, back home once again, my beloved is so tired, she forgets what she is doing while cooking and, that night, we have dress soup for dinner. I suppose we feel that supper is a great success, because next time we invite to dinner company we want to impress, we precede our dress soup with a bow-tie cocktail, a pair-of-pants salad, a main course consisting of underwear, and a shirt dessert. It seems only proper that, the next morning, when the beloved skips breakfast, she should simply explain that she feels "really stuffed."

Lurching Lunch

For some reason or other, I found myself running a little late; and so, to restore balance to my daily schedule, I decided to grab a sandwich. I really did have to grab it, too, because when I reached out to pick it up, it fled to the edge of the lunch counter, and I spent 20 minutes jumping all over the floor before I finally stepped on it and stopped it. Meanwhile, the pickle left the plate like a projectile and ended up out of reach, on the roof. For dessert, I had a cup of coffee which spilled all over my shirt, and a wedge of pie which, after I touched it with my fork, stuck in the wall like a spear. It was certainly a real time-saver, this lunch; and to express my thanks to the lunch counter and its clever manager, before I left, running out the door en route to the nearest French restaurant and a 10-course sit-down dinner, I gave the waitress a rather large tip.

The Sheet of Glass as Monocle

"The windows should be the focus of every house." The moment I read that illuminating statement, I dropped the interior-design magazine I had been reading all afternoon onto the floor, leaped to my feet, and rushed out of the room, back to the bathroom. In the medicine chest I found a bottle of Visine and an eyedropper, then ran back into the living-room, where, employing the eyedropper, I dripped Visine all over our two front picture windows. Then, with a bottle of Windex spray from the kitchen, and my polishing rag from the corner cabinet, I made haste to polish up those living-room windows until they shone every bit as brightly as any eyes. But clearly, something was wrong here; obviously, a finishing touch was necessary. So, rushing into our bedroom I grabbed the mascara from my wife's dressing-table, returned to the living-room and threw it all over all the curtains — concentrating of course on their fringes. Then, coughing and choking, I ran outside to catch my breath. While I was standing out there, I thought of yet another finishing touch which logic clearly dictated was both necessary and proper. After some rummaging around in the garage, I found a single rather large sheet of glass, carried it out to the front lawn, and propped it up with a stick to function out there as a monocle. But then I paused: Albeit in the interest of household beauty and decorum, was I perhaps making some mistake? What would my wife think? Mascara, monocle? — after all, who wants a homosexual as a house?

The Atmosphere of Amphitheatre

Whenever we turn on a faucet, the celebrated tube of water appears. We say "tube" because it appears not to be moving, it appears as likely to have been produced from the porcelain upwards as from the spigot downwards, as is the usual case. As for me, whenever I turn on any faucet, I satisfy my curiosity regarding its nature and character by simply telling myself that "a column is coming." This is why a person in a bathroom with both sink faucets running and the bathtub faucets dripping may be reminded of standing on a plantation veranda; and why it may be enough to walk through the laundryroom in the basement to experience a feeling reminiscent of standing among the ruins of Greek Temple architecture.

Oral Insomnia

It's another bad case of oral insomnia. Lips like feet kicking back the covers. Teeth like arms thrashing around. Ears ringing like stubbed toes. A burst of enthusiasm is indistinguishable from a wave of nausea after going to bed following a bad dinner. What sweet syrup will calm the stomach of the mind, will feed the mouth which still waters for metaphors? O, the shapely muse of modern food preparation techniques is entertaining us in our sleep, dressed only in a chef's hat. In the morning, we awake to find a sprig of parsley on the typewriter.

V. The Olympic Footsie Champion

The Olympic Footsie Champion

Throughout my life I've constantly been warned about playing footsie. First it was Joseph McCarthy warning against "playing footsie with the Communists." Then I was warned by a lesser religious leader against playing footsie with the devil. Then I was warned against playing footsie with the hearts of young women, and homosexuality. What is all this "footsie" people are always opposing? What is it about footsie that seems to be so frightening? Why is footsie even evil? Frankly, footsie sounds like great fun to me. In fact, I'd just love to spend part of my next vacation out in the local athletic fields, playing footsie. Yes, I think we should all go out right now and play some footsie! Perhaps we can even organize footsie teams, get local footsie matches listed in the Sports Section of *The New York Times*. Perhaps we can have footsie made a prerequisite in every junior-high-school and grade-school curriculum, footsie declared an intercollegiate sport, perhaps we can set up International Footsie Tournaments, even get them introduced into the Olympics? It's taken me a long time to come to this conclusion, but now I realize that the goal of my life is perhaps to appear on the world-wide footsie playing fields, and be addressed as "Hey Champ!"

The Foible

Here comes a genuine, card-carrying, sign-carrying Foible. Probably we all have one quite like it, too. It has spring in its feet, Christmas balls hanging from its tail; it has a moustache drawn on its face, one tooth blacked-out, and its chest is covered with old Christmas seals. It has a bunch of candy bars in its pocket to offer little children in exchange for whatever, also it's an occasional smoker, joker, and alcoholic. It detests graffiti in the subway, but not in the womens' or mens' room at the "Y." That is to say, it likes broad-brimmed hats, knows all the current baseball scores and batting averages; it likes its whiskey neat, its beer on ice; it hates coffee but loves tea, its steaks medium rare. It is Jewish or Buddhist, but celebrates both Easter and the Feast of the Assumption. Of course, it knows that the tomato is not a vegetable; it consistently rejects people with dirty fingernails or who confuse the difference between "imply" and "infer"; its favorite poet is Sidney Lanier's grandmother; it steals from Gristede's but never the A. & P. It doesn't like long hair below the collar, photographs of the dead, the sound of its own voice on the tape-recorder or telephone. It's a liberal, but it hates the Right. It is at the moment looking for a nice blonde Foible to marry, it wants to live in a little white house with a picket fence, and raise lots of other little Foibles just like it, unless two would be the maximum permitted by either decency or ecology. Something odd here: why a blonde Foible, with narrow ankles?—Despite its many redeeming, appealing qualities, it must be admitted: this Foible has a fetish. And unlike my fetish for accurate reportage and telling literal truth, this fetish gives some people the creeps. Here come The Creeps now, following the Foibles, knocking at your door by the thousands.

78

The Golf of Mexico

(1) When I was in Arizona recently, all I heard about was The Golf of Mexico this, the Golf of Mexico that, it's the most beautiful part of our country, you just must go see it immediately, it's so beautiful, etc. So I began to dream of making a trip south of the border some day to have a look at it. It must be wonderful, too, in the Southern fashion, I imagined; a golf range with no restrictions, everybody can have a hole in one, and also there is a hole for everyone in every Señorita. (2) Also, I should mention, I personally appreciate the fact that everybody there is supposed to be very tasteful. (3) Back and forth on the desert or lush green lawn go the little golf carts, the attendant caddies come running ahead of them with their machetes, to clear the way. . . . In the clubhouses, a lot of good fellowship among the Generals; jokes about women, peasants, animals. In one of the clubhouses, God gets a mention as slightly hilarious — that's when the waters of the Golf of Mexico rush in and cover the entire scene so that all you can see all of a sudden is a lot of golf clubs sticking up out of the water, coming up like periscopes, and waving around hysterically. And so my dream of a joyous visit to the Golf of Mexico evaporates, not to mention my expectations of ever again visiting Arizona.

Souvenir;
or, The Chinese-Made Mouse

I have this souvenir which a kind woman gave to me a long, long time ago. Even when she gave it to me, in the city of Cincinnati, and even though we only spent another six months there, she told me it was meant to be a souvenir. She gave it to me, I remember, at the very height of what I suppose might best be termed the craziest kind of passion — I remember, at the time, that we were actually sharing feelings mutually reciprocated! — and this was to be signified by this little stuffed toy which she slipped under my pillow early one morning. Then she left. True, it's only a small felt mouse. Perhaps I also ought to say that the workmanship is really fantastic — perfect bristle whiskers, onyx eyes, a tail with realistically mouselike limpness and soft white fur, from which a slightly greyer nose just juts out, jet-black at the very tip. But what am I saying? What would that mean? As if the meaning of this gift were in the least determined by the level of workmanship at the local "Arts-and-Crafts Shoppe" in Peking, where the tag said the mouse was made. Except as a reflection of the immediate ambitions of the local Mayor or Chamber of Commerce chief, or Chairman or President, isn't such a souvenir really retained not so much to reassure us of the virtues of the region where we acquired it, however impressive, but simply to reassure us about life by reminding us that once we were in some kind of pleasant place, one that moved us much, wherever it was? Once in Tijuana I bought myself a Mexican hat. In Majorca once I bought a large, colorful bowl. In Paris I bought a toy Eiffel Tower to use as an ashtray. Whenever I see any of them they make me happy about having been some place lovely, and remind me of the joy of possibly returning. But what about this mouse? I got it a long, long time ago, around 1975. It might as well have been 1935. To get back to its particular native land you need more than a passport.

How to Disembark from a Lark

(1) The little ladder has been placed in position and everybody is climbing up the staircase onto its back. And, look, already its wings are beginning to beat in anticipation! Little clouds of dust are coming out from both sides now. Now, everybody is seated in neat rows on its back and set for flight. This is precisely when you begin to experience, for some unknown reason, a certain feeling of uneasiness. So you begin to wonder: is this lark you are on truly prudent? No: logic has not deserted you yet! At once, displaying your customary perspicacity, you start to disembark. You grab your hat, you grab your coat, you grab your luggage and lorgnette, and begin to call out for the porter to throw your suitcases out from beneath the pinfeathers. But suddenly you sense waves of disapproval beginning to radiate your way. "Oh, what a spoil-sport," somebody cries out from beneath the beak, "in such a hurry to depart, and the trip only just begun!" Mumbles are coming from the smoking-lounge! The words "party pooper" a rumor in the Piano Bar! But still, your customary control and logic continue to dominate. For, as the lark begins to run across the field, you realize, with perfect lucidity, that if you're ever going to leave this lark, this could be your last chance right now! Abandoning your luggage, abandoning the little ladder, abandoning everything but your understanding, you fling yourself off into space, into the very teeth of the breeze, just beneath the snap of its beak, and the whizz of its retracting legs. For fully five minutes after touchdown you tumble around on the runway in the wake of its windy slipstream. (2) No, you think. In your most lucid moments of all, you wonder whether once a person is committed to such a venture, it is ever in fact truly prudent to disembark from a lark.

The Tiny Sisyphus and the Dung Beetle

One afternoon a tiny Sisyphus and a dung beetle met as they were conducting their activities on the slope of the same hill. "What have you got there?" asked the dung beetle, looming large over Sisyphus, towering by reason of his enormous moral stature. "I have here the Impossible — my fate, my destiny, my burden, and my pain," said Sisyphus. The dung beetle just laughed. "And what responsibility have you got there?" Sisyphus asked. "Shit," said the dung beetle, and rolled merrily away up the hill. The astonished Sisyphus, on the other hand, fell over backwards like a cockroach, while his great burden rolled all the way back down the hill as far as the local community college.

An Immense Gosling

"That certainly is an immense gosling!" Becky exclaimed, sitting at the picture window. "Just look at it now, coming down the road!" And sure enough, from her windowseat, she saw a rather large wingtip come passing by the window, with its big neck thick as a question mark. Transported by joy, Becky went jumping up and down on her windowseat. Imagine her surprise when the question mark flattened to an exclamation point; when the beak stuck in the window, picked up Becky by her silken underdrawers, and dropped her flat on the floor, fracturing her coccyx. "My," Becky exclaimed, as she ended her tale while laughing and brandishing her brandy bottle, "that certainly was a big pisser!" "Oh, no, it was an immense gosling, you mean," I corrected her from the neighboring hospital bed. "Tell me the whole story one more time," I added, climbing in next to her and pulling the covers up over both of us. This more or less represents the important part of this story, as relates to the urgent subject of immense goslings.

Tale

When the alarm went off, Freddie jumped a foot. How so? Well, Freddie just happened to be walking around nude in the forest, when this sweet young cheerleader in short skirts whom Freddie had been fantasizing about for many years happened to go past; and just as the radar alarm in her pocketbook went off, notifying her that there was a stranger somewhere near, he jumped on her. Her name was Ms. Linda Foote. And that's how Freddie came to jump a foot. Believe me, there is a much more radical and relevant version of this tale in my notebook: it's about how a Foot jumped the freddie.

Celebrated Things

"Ah, so you're the celebrated poet," my ironical uncle hissed at me from underneath a leaf of his coffeetable. But by this time I knew how to respond to him; I wasn't speaking to him. How appropriate it would be, I thought, if all the people who aren't too careful about language anyway were to begin to react exactly the way such an uncle does; such an uncle is one who regards himself as the soul of neatness yet who is fully capable of confusing the term "celebrated" with the term "well-known." So that all over town, at the height of their enthusiasm, people in after-hours clubs who had been educated as had my uncle would be busy raising their glasses to toast "the celebrated turds," "the celebrated rat-poison," and best and most celebrated of all, "the celebrated unpleasantness." Simultaneously, the famous unknown soldier would arise, take a taxi back across the city from the cemetery, and become the toast of the town; except that he will already be so celebrated that even his initial appearance will make everybody sick with repetition. Then, while the Gobi desert becomes celebrated by being irrigated with the enthusiasms of travel folders, Greta Garbo's appearance will cause a gossip-columnist to snore. And, after all these celebrations mistaking noxious for notorious, my ironical uncle's mind will be certified, by the celebrated Association for Bad Poetry and Worse Politics, "significant"; perhaps, even, "relevant."

New Year's Resolutions

Yes, I'll admit that I have been sinful. For one full year I had been having a love affair with the number four. That was back in 1974. But we all love best what we know best! All that time, 1975 was practically a mere cipher to me. Then, suddenly, the affair was over. But, oh, the love poems I wrote! Beautiful verses, believe me; flowing verses that wrung the heart. But that's been over for some time now — for nearly six years in fact. True, I remained fundamentally faithful to the one I am wedded to, the number 19. Then again, lately I envisioned an 8, and she really caught my eye. Also a zero: that is, a real child. Somewhat underaged, even. My difficulties obviously get deeper every day. In addition to that, I must confess that the year 2000 always did give me an erection. My pornography is the next century.

January 1, 1980

Orders from Beyond

(1) I don't know about your boss, but my particular employer is certainly exacting. For example: Not too long ago the orders came down from above: no more of this sloppy filing, no more of these simpleminded primordial rectangles and manilla folders. From now on everything you file information on has to be made of the same material you are filing the information about: and also, it has to be in the same shape as the thing you are filing the information about. Thus (the boss told me), information on metals must be made out of metal, plaster out of plaster, and water out of water. Only information on manila file folders can henceforth be filed in manila file folders. "Sure, boss," I said. (2) As luck would have it, the first subject I was supposed to manufacture a file for, was an octopus. It was only a partial success, at best. Also, after I manufactured this first file, the octopus took a liking to me, grabbed me and hugged me like a mother. A sympathetic office-boy had to separate us. (3) The second subject was "heavy winds," and these blew me all over the room. Even my former file folders, which I had been relying on just in case of emergency, became somewhat of a mess. (4) The third subject the boss asked me to file was information on the nature of the universe. By the time I finished this one, a full week plus a weekend of overtime had passed; but on the eighth day, I rested.

The Search for the Source

I can't imagine where it comes from, but surely there must be a source for this all, somewhere. True, streams can be seen sometimes, using a dowsing-rod, or even if you simply look carefully under rocks with a flashlight at midnight; but this source isn't so easy to find. In fact, the harder you look, the more it disappears; and all you can think about is that since it doesn't seem to be prevalent anywhere near the surface, perhaps it's someplace else, perhaps it's down at the center of the earth somewhere, who knows? It's not an easy thing to grasp, perhaps it's better to skip the entire subject, why am I bothering to write this all down, anyway? Here I am with a poetry almost empty of encouraging imagery. On the other hand, nothing you can do can change what you know. Last week, for example, there was a major critic from Milwaukee who said (making a rich metaphor) that he found my inspiration "a bit dry"; not to mention my wife. *He* meant that the flow was always awful. God knows what *she* meant. I suppose that all I'm supposed to have left is a lot of water pouring all over my face. But maybe that's enough, though; maybe that's all the source there ever was or will be; maybe I've found it now, whether I'm laughing or crying now, maybe I can truthfully say at last that I've never ever been happier.